How to Kayak

An Introduction to Kayaking for Beginners

Kenneth Martin

Copyright © 2017 by Kenneth Martin

All rights reserved.

No part of this publication may be reproduced, distributed, or transmitted in any form or by any means, including photocopying, recording, or other electronic or mechanical methods, without the prior written permission of the publisher, except in the case of brief quotations embodied in critical reviews.

While the publisher and author have used their best efforts in preparing this book, they make no representations or warranties with respect to the accuracy or completeness of the content of this book.

The advice and strategies contained herein may not be suitable for your situation. You should consult with a professional where appropriate.

Neither the publisher, nor contributors / authors shall be liable for any damages, including but not limited to special, incidental, consequential, or other damages.

Acknowledgement

Getting a book written, proofed and published is no small job. I want to thank the many people that were instrumental in bringing this idea to life. In particular, I would like to thank friends and family for helping me with the selection, editing and proofreading of this book.

Table of Contents

Introduction	v
Chapter 1: Safety First	1
Chapter 2: Basic Kayak Terms	3
Chapter 3: Kayak Types	5
Chapter 4: Kayak Parts	8
Chapter 5: Kayak Paddles	11
Chapter 6: Kayak Paddling	13
Chapter 7: Launching and Landing a Kayak	19
Chapter 8: Transporting your Kayak and Things	22
Chapter 9: Right of Way	25
Chapter 10: Universal Communication	28
Chapter 11: Capsizing and Righting	30
Chapter 12: Self-Rescue	34
Conclusion	36

How To Kayak

Introduction

Have you ever wanted to learn how to kayak? Here is your chance to learn kayaking.

Steeped in tradition that traces back to the Inuit, kayaking has evolved from a necessity into a fun and heart healthy recreation and sport.

Regardless of the many differences in size and shape, kayaks are usually driven by one person with a paddle sitting in its cockpit.

Although this book is by no means an exhaustive look at the world of kayaking, it's a great starting point for beginners that will help you easily master the kayaking fundamentals you will need to confidently get you out on the water. This book was written was written as a concise and practical guide designed to get you started and involved.

How to Kayak: An Introduction to Kayaking for Beginners, covers the essentials step-by-step without overwhelming you with intimidating diagrams and lists. It walks you through everything you need to know to become a competent and responsible paddler.

How To Kayak

Getting out on the water is easier than you think. We have taken the intimidation out and given you the tools to get out there Kayaking on your first day!

In short, once you have read this book you should be familiar with:

- **General safety & etiquette;**
- **How to launch;**
- **How to make the kayak go where you want;**
- **How to right a capsized kayak;**
- **And much more!**

Be safe & have fun!

Chapter 1: Safety First

When you go kayaking it is important to know some things about safety. To begin with you should know how to swim, wear a PFD and make sure to check the weather. Needless to say, on sunny days don't forget the sunscreen, on cold days don't forget your cold weather gear. If you are going to be whitewater kayaking, put on a helmet. Check your equipment before heading out. Know a thing or two about water safety and first aid. Just make sure to use common sense. Remember accidents happen when you least expect them.

Kayaking safety involves a wide range of activities and the use of important safety gear and equipment. As a rule of thumb, you should consider the following:

1. **Take a Course** -Whether it's for safety or general skill development, an ACA on-water instruction course will provide the information you need for kayaking or safety & rescue.

2. **Wear your Lifejacket** -You are going to capsize and swim occasionally when paddling a kayak. It is par for the course and part of the process. You should learn as much as you can about just how important PFDs are.

3. **Cold Water Safety** – Cold water is very dangerous. The most deadly situation you can encounter is becoming wet and not being able to get dry or warm. Hypothermia sets in very quickly, so in colder weather and especially in colder water, it is essential to be prepared with securely stowed dry clothing and extra layers for additional protection.

4. You need to learn the **Rules of the Road** – If you are on active waterways you should know who has the right of way and how to pass.

5. **Safety Check** – Make sure to be reasonable and use a degree of common sense. This doesn't just mean being prepared with a First Aid Kit and ensuring that everything is in working order, it means knowing your limitations. If you can't swim, I don't recommend kayaking. If you aren't in shape, then you may want to start a fitness regimen. If you are new, don't shoot the rapids. Know your limits and everything will fall into place.

Chapter 2: Basic Kayak Terms

Paddling is a unique sport and recreation that is steeped in tradition and dates back centuries in North America. Before getting started, it is important to become familiar with common boating terminology. As you add to your vocabulary, you are going to find that some of the terms make perfect sense, while others may seem a bit arbitrary.

Aside from the terms used for the different parts of the boat, there are also certain terms that we commonly use while on the water. Some of these basic paddling terms are:

Aft: Back part of boat.

Astern: Back part of boat.

Amidship: Center of boat.

Ballast: Weight that lowers center of gravity and adds stability.

Bow: Front part of the boat.

Forward: Ahead; toward the front of the Boat.

Leeward: This is also called 'Lee'. This is the direction to which the wind is blowing, downwind.

Offside: Direction of a maneuver in which the craft moves away from the bow; designated paddling side.

Onside: Direction of a maneuver in which the craft moves toward the bow; designated paddling side

Port: When you are facing the bow (the front of the boat) the side to your left is the port side.

Powerface: Side of paddle blade pressed against the water during a forward stroke.

Spraydeck (sprayskirt): Neoprene or nylon covering worn around the waist and attached to the cockpit to keep water out of the kayak.

Starboard: Starboard is the right side of the boat when facing the bow.

Stern: Back part of boat.

Trim: Balanced from end to end and side to side.

Windward: As the name might imply, windward is the direction from which the wind is blowing, upwind.

Chapter 3: Kayak Types

I thought I would start you off on your introduction into kayaking by identifying some of the basic kayak types, so that when you do get on the water you will be able to readily pick out the different types. Like everything else kayaks come in many shapes and sizes.

In general, kayaks will fall into three specific types. These are the touring kayak, the whitewater kayak and the recreational kayak.

Touring kayak:

Touring kayaks are better-performing and more versatile than recreational kayaks, though they're typically more expensive. The with the touring kayak you can travel long distances in open water, and handle in rough conditions.

They have more storage space (especially multiday boats) and bulkheads with sealed hatches enhance safety. These compartments trap air, which gives the kayak flotation even if the cockpit fills with water.

Touring kayaks are usually 12 to 17 feet (3.7 to 5.18 m) feet long, and their hulls are shaped to increase lift in waves and rough water. Most have a tracking system such as a skeg or rudder, or a combination of the two.

Cockpits are likely to be built for paddling efficiency and use with a spray skirt, which may feel confining to some.

Touring kayaks can be made of plastic or a lightweight and durable composite blend.

<u>Whitewater kayak:</u>

Whitewater kayaks are rotomolded in a semi-rigid, high impact plastic, usually polyethylene. Careful construction ensures that the boat remains structurally sound when subjected to fast-moving water.

The plastic hull allows these kayaks to bounce off rocks without leaking, although they scratch and eventually wear through with enough use. Whitewater kayaks range from 4 to 10 feet (1.2 to 3.0 m) long.

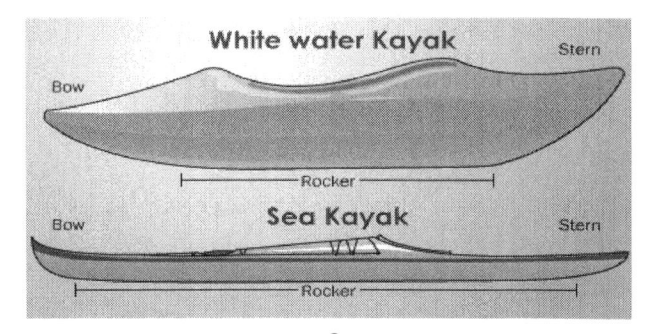

Recreational kayak:

Recreational kayaks are designed for the casual paddler interested in fishing, photography, or a peaceful paddle on a lake, flatwater stream or protected salt water away from strong ocean waves.

These boats presently make up the largest segment of kayak sales. Compared to other kayaks, recreational kayaks have a larger cockpit for easier entry and exit and a wider beam (27–36 inches (69–91 cm)) for more stability. They are generally less than 12 feet (3.7 m) in length and have limited cargo capacity. Less expensive materials like polyethylene and fewer options keep these boats relatively inexpensive.

Most kayak clubs offer introductory instruction in recreational boats. They do not perform as well in the sea. The recreational kayak is usually a type of touring kayak.

Chapter 4: Kayak Parts

Kayaks are different from canoes by virtue of their narrower, lower shape and the fact that they are enclosed. The basic Inuit kayak is the basis for today's kayak while the necessities dictated by recreational and whitewater uses have shortened and narrowed the boat. A kayak is propelled with a paddle that has a blade on each end whereas there is only one on a canoe paddle. Different hull shapes and edge designs serve different purposes such as speed, maneuverability and stability.

Although kayaks come in a great variety of lengths and widths, they all share some common characteristics. For example, some of these common features are the cockpit, the deck, the hatches and the handles.

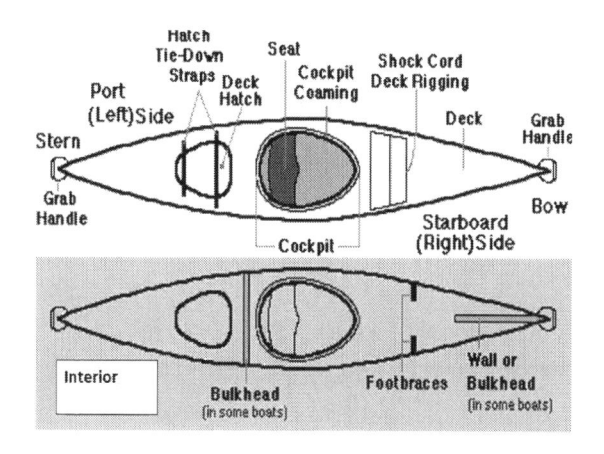

Bow: Front of the boat.

Beam: Width of the boat.

Bulkhead: Used to reinforce craft structure.

Cockpit: Opening where the paddler sits.

Cockpit Coaming: Watertight material around the rim of the cockpit.

Deck: Top of the kayak.

Footbraces: Pegs where you place your feet.

Handle: Rope loop and handle that lets you hold on to the end of the kayak, attach a towline, or tie the kayak on a car top rack or other transport.

Hatch: Compartment used for storing gear.

Port: The left side of the boat.

Rigging: Rigging can be a practical and useful addition to your boat. Your forward deck rigging is a useful place for your water bottle, small tackle box or a place to rest the paddle . The stern deck rigging is required for setting up a paddle float self-rescue and carrying your paddle float and pump.

Seat: Inside the cockpit where the paddler sits.

Starboard: Right side of the boat.

Stern: Back part of the boat.

Chapter 5: Kayak Paddles

Kayak paddles are long and double bladed. In general, there are two types of kayak paddles: touring and whitewater.

Whitewater paddles have a rigid shaft, wide blades, and typically are feathered (blades set at an angle to each other). This allows the paddler to have control while traveling through rapids. On the other hand, Touring paddles are designed for efficiency and comfort and are good for traveling. They have a more narrow and smaller blade. Blades may be cupped (spoon) or flat. Flat blades are better for beginners.

Kayak paddles have either right-hand or left-hand control. This allows a designated hand to maintain a firm grasp on the paddle while controlling the angle of the blades. It also allows the shaft to rotate within the other hand between strokes and maintain a firm grasp during the stroke. Hand control is determined by the powerface of the blade. For example, if the power stroke is on the right side of the kayak, and the powerface of the opposite blade is facing up, then it is a right-hand control paddle. Most paddles sold are right-hand control. Straight and bent shafts also are available in kayak paddles. Most beginners use straight shafts. There are two throats and tips in a kayak paddle because they are double bladed.

Sizing

When sizing a kayak paddle, consider the type of paddling you will be doing, the width of the kayak, and your torso length. A general rule is that an average size paddler (5'2" - 6'2") in an average sized solo boat can use a 200-220 cm (80-88 inches) paddle.

Chapter 6: Kayak Paddling

Kayaks are typically solo crafts where the paddler has a paddle with a double blade. The double blade of the kayak paddle allows kayakers to paddle on both sides without having to switch. You are, in effect, the engine room of the boat with the power being provided by the rotation of your torso and shoulders.

Paddling Positions

Paddlers should sit straight when kayaking. This allows a broader range of movement and an increase in strength to perform strokes and maneuvers.

Boat lean helps kayakers feel the stability of their craft. It occurs when a paddler pulls one knee up, while simultaneously pushing down with the opposite hip and keeping his body weight above the kayak. This transfers weight to the hip and allows the paddler to balance on that hip. This will move the craft underneath him.

Paddling a kayak involves a push-pull action against the paddle. When going forward, kayakers punch out with their upper arms and pull back with their lower arms. This creates a need for kayakers to rotate their body, while keeping their trunk and shoulders facing their hands.

Holding the Paddle

Grip the paddle in the palm of your hands rather than your fingers. This makes it easier to cock your wrists and gives you better control over the paddle. Your hands should be at a greater width than your shoulders. Your elbows are at a 90° angle to your forearms, which are approximately a 70° to 90° angle to the paddle shaft. An easy way for beginner kayakers to remember their hand position is to tape their proper grip location on the paddle.

Basic Strokes

Kayak strokes are straightforward. When the paddle is planted in the water and the paddler pulls, she is pulling herself and the kayak along. The power in kayak strokes comes from the push of the upper hand, twist of the torso, and pull of the lower hand. The use of all three will provide smooth, quick, strong strokes. In general, there are forward stoke, the backward stroke, the forward sweep stroke, the backward sweep stroke, the draw stroke and the stop.

Forward Stroke

The forward stroke moves the kayak forward. In order to execute proper forward stroke the blade should be completely in the water and parallel to the centerline. The paddler's stroke should not cross the centerline as this makes the stoke too long and may cause the boat to turn. The stroke should look something like this:

- The paddler's torso rotates with the right shoulder forward and the blade inserted in the water close to the kayak.
- Next, the upper hand punches out toward the bow handle, while the lower are pulls, rotating the paddler's body. The upper hand will continue to full extension of the arm, while the upper body follows through for full rotation. The lower hand will stop at your hip.
- Then, the paddle will be removed from the water by quickly lifting your wrist and elbow to shoulder level allowing for a quick and easy recovery of the blade. Now, with the torso rotated with the left shoulder forward and ready to repeat the motion from you left. Then, back to the right. Then left. In so doing the kayak in propelled forward.

Back stroke

The back stroke is much like the forward stroke, but in reverse. In other words, it would be akin to walking backward. Naturally, the back stoke move the boat backward. In the back stroke, the grip stay s the same as the forward stroke and the paddle should stay parallel to centerline. In essence, it will look like this:

- You will rotate your left shoulder with torso as much as possible and place the paddle as far back as practical.
- Next, the lower hand pushes forward while the upper hand pulls back. The right arm moves to paddler's shoulder. Then, this motion is repeated from the right side.

Forward sweep stroke

The forward sweep stroke is used as a primary means to turn the kayak. It will turn the bow of the kayak the opposite direction paddled while maintaining forward motion.

For a specific turn, you reach forward as far as possible and stick the blade into the water. Instead of drawing the paddle along the side of the kayak, you will reach out with a straight lower arm and pull the paddle back in an arc.

As the water blade is drawing back close to the stern of the kayak, the paddle should be flipped and raised from the water. If the boat has remained stable and the blade comes out of the water cleanly, the kayak will continue to turn.

Reverse sweep stroke

This is essentially the reverse of the forward sweep stroke that will slow the kayak. It will turn the craft to the side it is performed on. Without changing your grip on the paddle like we had discussed with the backward stroke, you place the blade into the water as far back as possible, rotating your torso and shoulders for the best extension.

With rotation from the torso, draw the water blade forward in a wide arc removing it from the water before hitting the bow of the boat. Frequently, the forward and reverse sweep strokes are used together to make a boat turn more quickly.

Draw stroke

The draw stroke pulls the boat sideways. It is executed by turning the body toward the direction in which you want to move. Simply, extend the paddle out as far from the edge of the kayak and make sure the blade is turned toward the kayak before inserting in the water. The paddler then pulls the boat to the blade using both arms and keeping the paddle nearly vertical.

The lower hand applies much of the force. The stroke ends when the blade is near the craft. The blade is then lifted out of the water and placed in the position that you started in. That's, if you need to repeat.

Stopping:

Lastly, simply ceasing to paddle will not stop a kayak. Stopping it requires you to stick the blade into the water right at your side with the blade perpendicular to the kayak. Try to hold the paddle straight until the resistance begins to turn the kayak. Quickly stick the paddle into the water at the other side and repeat the procedure until you have stopped.

Chapter 7: Launching and Landing a Kayak

So now you know how to make your Kayak go with the various paddle stroke, let's finally turn our attention to getting on the water. Aside from the seal launch which is a very advanced launch method usually used in whitewater kayaking and some cool and nifty slips, there are three main launchings: directly from the beach area, from the edge of the water and from a dock.

Beach entry

One of the easiest ways to get into the kayak is to place the bow of the kayak straight into the water with the stern still resting on the beach. Then, sit on back of the deck, put your feet into the cockpit and slide in until you are properly seated. Once comfortably seated, you should then rock and sift your weight side to side while pushing yourself forward with the paddle until afloat. Remember kayaks have very little draft.

Edge of water entry

The next entry type is from the edge of a river or stream. Ensure that the kayak is parallel with the land / edge . Place the kayak's paddle across the back of the cockpit and the other half of the paddle rests on the land. With much of your weight on the paddle and across the back of the cockpit, you then from a crouching position on the shore shift yourself into the cockpit and slide in.

Dock entry

When launching the kayak from a dock the technique is relatively the same as the edge of water entry. The only difference is that you may have to compensate for the height of the dock.

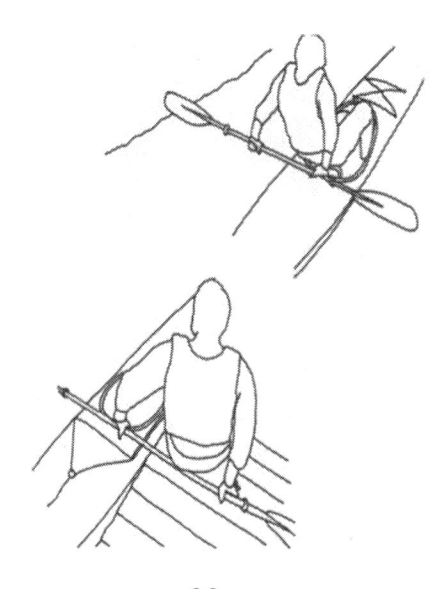

Please visit the following link for a demonstration:

https://www.youtube.com/watch?v=UqrtZJkA-qo

Landing

When landing you simply reverse the steps outlined above. Just remember that when you approach you must be wary of obstructions and ensure that you don't run aground.

Normally these techniques are taught in class and practiced in the calmest of conditions or in pools so that they become second nature to the newly minted paddler.

Chapter 8: Transporting your Kayak and Things

When you buy a kayak you are going to need to consider how to get it from the store to your house and more importantly from your house to the water. Perhaps you'll be part of a club that may help you with this.

To get the kayak from point A to B, there are special roof racks specifically designed for this task. Although there are trolleys, I have been using a standard J-Rack System for transport to and from the site. This will require that you hoist the craft to the roof of your car and place the kayak in the crook of the J on its side with the cockpit outward and covered to keep the air from scooping it and to keep your paddles and gear that you may have stowed safely within. Once it is positioned, secure the boat with special straps designed just for the task.

Another method that I have retired is the use of specialized saddles/ boots that I would affix to the roof of my Subaru. I literally would bring it to the rear of the car and center the boat in line with the rack and push it up until properly positioned. Then I would secure it with specialized strap and rope to ensure that it was secure. You can never have enough rope.

Kayaks are very lightweight and can be manipulated by one person although awkwardly. In this manner, the cockpit rim can be placed on your shoulder and walked to the water. That aside, however, I would highly recommend that you don't do this and have another person help you.

How To Kayak

Two people are definitely better than one when it comes to this! The handles on the bow and stern make this a relatively easy endeavor.

Chapter 9: Right of Way

Like cars, kayaks must respect the rules of the road or as the case is -- water. This is very important when you are sharing the water with swimmers and other boaters.

As a rule of thumb, any boat with more maneuverability must give way to any boat with less maneuverability.

Collisions occur between boats more often than you might think. Most of the time bigger boats will not even see you. Since kayaks are very maneuverable, it is usually up to us to keep clear and give way to larger vessels.

When in a narrow channel with other boats, the kayaker should stay to the shore-side of navigational markers or buoys and cross traffic at a right angle and as quickly as possible and only if trying to reach port or avoid danger. There are shipping lanes marked on charts, and less formal but equally real lanes where ferries run. Know where the shipping lanes and the ferry runs are, and avoid them! If you are in a fog it is best to also have a horn or whistle.

When meeting a boat head-on, you should let it pass to your left, as should they. Make a definitive course correction so they have no doubt as to which way you are headed. If someone is approaching from your stern, you must maintain your course, and they must avoid you. You still must pay close attention to traffic from your stern, because they might not be able to see you below their bow. Boats entering waterways from slips or marinas will not see you, and you must exercise caution in those situations.

Whenever two boats come close to each other, the rules designate one as the stand-on vessel and the other as the give-way vessel. In general, a kayak will always give way to:

- A disabled vessel or a vessel not under command;
- vessels restricted in their ability to maneuver;
- A vessel restricted by draft;
- A vessel engaged in fishing.

Kayak vs. Powerboat

Powerboats cause a lot of headaches as they oftentimes don't know the rules of the road and may cross your path. In most situations the powerboat/ watercraft should give way to you and do their best to avoid you, but this isn't always the case. Be careful and alert when they are in your vicinity as they can be on you quickly and may leave you in their wake.

While there are some situations where the kayak has right-of-way, you cannot assume that other boaters are able to see you or even know the rules. In addition to being safe and courteous with other boaters, just remember to use a hefty dose of common sense.

Chapter 10: Universal Communication

I thought it proper since we just finished the Rules of the Road to continue on this theme and introduce you to the universal communication that kayaks use. There are five signals altogether. There are Stop, Distress/ Emergency, All Clear, Directions and Are you OK?

Stop:

Using both hands hold the paddle straight up over your head. Other people behind you should stop and wait for further signals from you.

Distress/ Emergency/ Help:

The kayaker should blow three whistle blasts. There should be a a whistle or horn aboard oe attached to your pdf. Hold the paddle up vertically and wave it from side to side to indicate distress. All others should remain at distance unless trained in emergency response.

All Clear:

The paddle supported by one hand is held straight up in the air.

How To Kayak

Directions:

Hold the paddle vertically and indicate the direction you want to head out in. The way should be clear and free from obstacles.

Common Paddle Signals

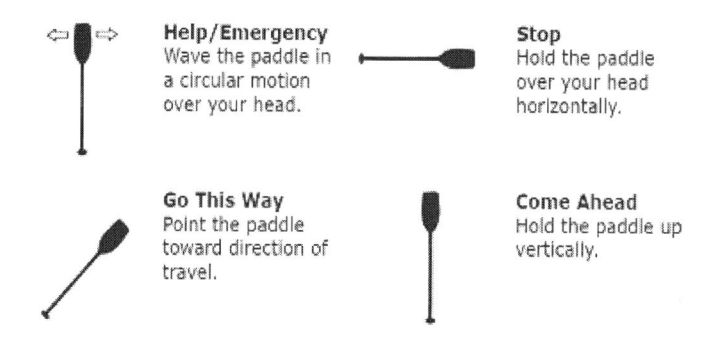

Help/Emergency
Wave the paddle in a circular motion over your head.

Stop
Hold the paddle over your head horizontally.

Go This Way
Point the paddle toward direction of travel.

Come Ahead
Hold the paddle up vertically.

Are you OK?

With your hands, point to the person in question and tap three times on top of your head/ helmet.

Chapter 11: Capsizing and Righting

Now that you've mastered the right way, how to use the paddle, how to turn a kayak, how to stop a kayak, it is time to learn something more advanced. Every seasoned kayaker will experience capsizing one day. It is not if it is going to happen. It is more a matter of when. It's an essential part of the experience, whether you do it on purpose or for fun, you have to try capsizing at least once to really complete your kayaking experience and to prepare yourself.

The easiest way to recover your kayak after capsizing is employing a technique called the Eskimo Roll.

1. If your kayak is going to fully capsize, you will need to anticipate it. Before you're completely submerged you need to bring your paddle parallel the kayak, rolling your wrist forward.

2. As the kayak is upside down, turn the paddle and reach out to grab the water, bringing your paddle up near the surface of the water.

3. Use your hips to allow you to flip the kayak back upright. This is the most important part. Your arms are not the key part of allowing you to turn back up. They only help position the paddle. Your hips are the ones doing the work here.

While you are underwater, you need to throw your hips to the right and to the left, almost as if you are wiggling in your seat. This is the momentum that is going to allow your kayak to turn back upright.

After this, you should have already recovered your capsized kayak. You need to practice this move a couple times before you can truly master it. It is essential to know this move when you're out kayaking because you never know when you might capsize and you will need to put these skills to test. Safety is truly of utmost importance when you're out at in the open sea.

Please visit the following link for a demonstration:

https://www.youtube.com/watch?v=117MH2CFc8o

Falling out of your seat while capsizing

How To Kayak

If you should fall out of the cockpit while kayaking, make sure to not to panic and stay with the boat.

1. Firstly, you will have to return your kayak into an upright position. Simply reach under your kayak and grab on to both sides of the cockpit rim to push it over and flip it upright.

2. Once your kayak is upright, you'll have to reach across to the opposite side of it and simply pull your whole body up and onto the kayak, as if you were getting out of a swimming pool.

3. Now that you're on the kayak again, you need to position yourself back into your sitting position by flipping your body over and sliding yourself back into your seat.

You now know how to get back onto your kayak once you've capsized whether be it while still in the kayak or if you fell out of the kayak.

At the end of the day, you need to be careful when you do this because waters can be rather unpredictable. Although recovering from a capsized kayak can be quite fun to practice, never do it unsupervised.

Normally these techniques are taught in class and practiced in the calmest of conditions or in pools so that they become second nature to the newly minted paddler.

Chapter 12: Self-Rescue

In the last chapter, we covered how to get back into the kayak unaided. Sometimes the kayaks don't allow for a smooth re-entry due to the beam of the craft or other reasons. In this case, we would use a paddle float to help us get back on board which is normally stowed forward under the bow bungees. Simply put, they are inflatable sleeves that fit around one end of the paddle. The end that is inflated floats on the water white the other end of the paddle is placed or rather stuck under the bungees aft of the cockpit forming an outrigger. This should give you enough leverage and stabilization to be able to get back into the cockpit.

Sometimes, however, the kayak has taken on too much water and you need to use your pump which is also stowed in an easily accessible place like under the bow bungees. Typically, kayaks are designed to convey a 235lb person. 1 pint of water weighs in at a pound. Therefore, you can see how heavy a waterlogged kayak may become. Before you slide back into the cockpit try to get as much water out as you can.

Normally this technique is taught in class and practiced in the calmest of conditions or in pools so that they become second nature to the newly minted paddler.

Please visit the following link for a demonstration:

https://www.youtube.com/watch?v=hkj2S4yxoQI

Conclusion

I have taken you through a lot of information in the preceding chapters. It is going to take some time to process. Kayaking is all about practice. Don't worry, it will all come together.

I had a lot of goals when I set out to write this book, but the most important was to shed light on kayaking and to get you out on the water.

Whether you have never been kayaking or would like to know enough to join a local paddle club or you plan on getting your own kayak, this book has something for you.

I hope you have found this book to be a useful tool in gaining a better understanding of just what kayaking is all about.

I have taken you through a lot about kayaking and how it works. You know how to paddle, you know how to launch and land, you know how to right yourself, should you capsize. In short: you are ready!

Thank you for the time you took to read this book.

Now, get on the water with confidence!

Have fun & be safe!

Made in the USA
Middletown, DE
25 August 2018